THE TEN PERSONALITY TYPES

YOU CAN CHOOSE FROM FOR YOUR SUCCESS

N. SHRETH CHONGTHAM | PH.D.

Made with ♥ on the Notion Press Platform
www.notionpress.com

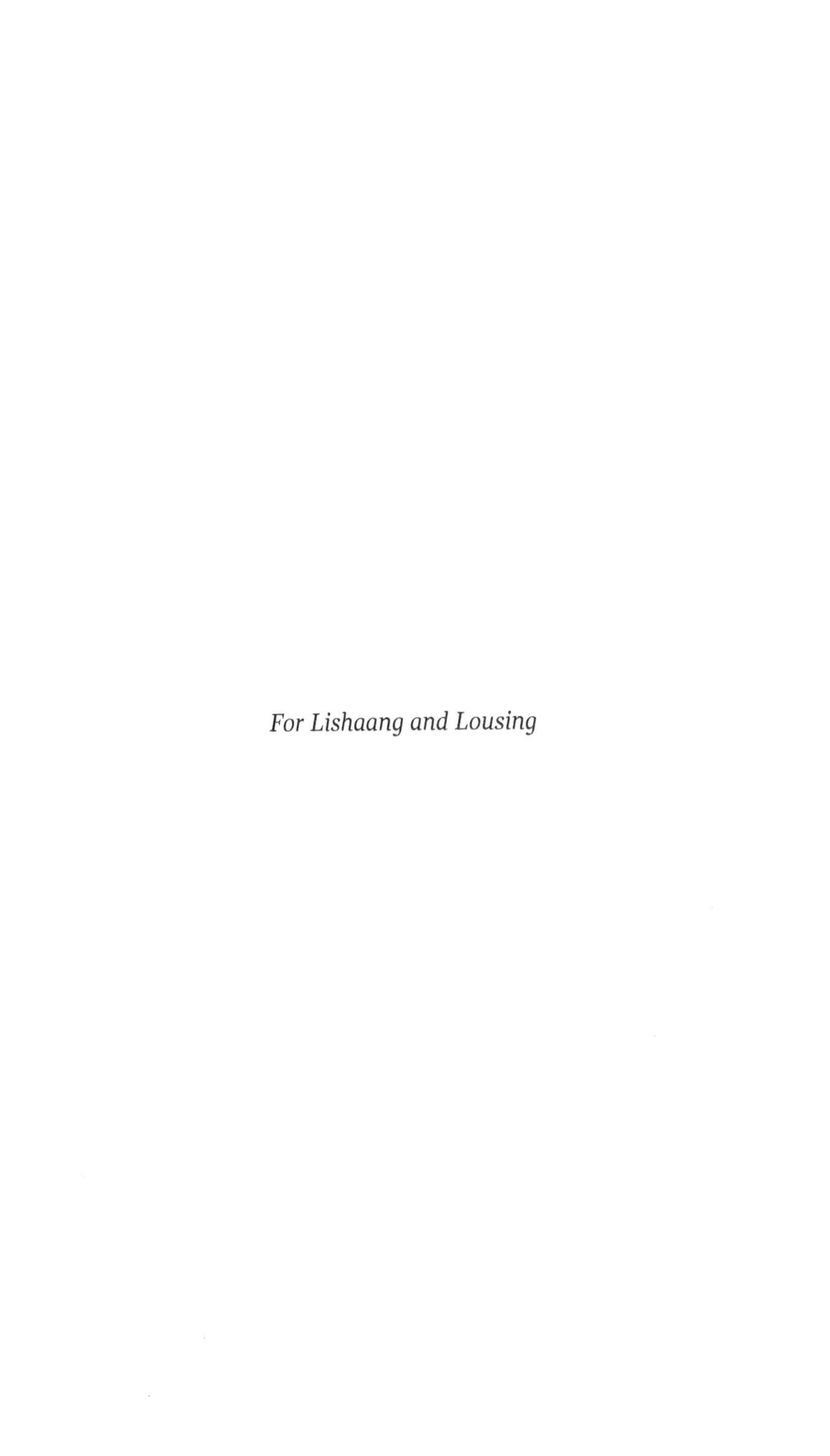

For Lishaang and Lousing

Contents

Preface

Hello!

My name is N. Shreth Chongtham.

Writing has always been my thing. After the success of 'Para Tara', a self-help book in Manipuri, I am writing the second installment of the same book. During this write-up, I came upon various types of personalities - directly and through book. I have always been fascinated by the different types of people we meet daily. This made me realised I missed out writing about personality type.

For this I am greatly influenced by the unexpected source of motivation, a book called Word Power Made Easy.

You will find most of the content of this book highly influenced by that book. My aim is to make the readers analyse their personality and, if possible change for good.

Although my book is intended for the young adults, I hope it will not be shun by men and women because it's them that need the CHANGE.

I hope to hear if the book is useful. Feel free to drop a mail at shrethchongtham@gmail.com

Acknowledgements

I take this opportunity to thank many people of my life. Their perpetual support and unending love makes me what I am today. I thank all of you. There is no way I can name all of them or hope to remember all the people who helped me in this journey, but I now I am grateful to all these wonderful people.

My heartfelt gratitude goes to my Dronarcharyas, O. Henry and Paulo Coelho. This book is able to see the light of the day due to these wonderful writers who motivates me. My mentors and guide for lifetime - Dr. S. John William, (L) Prof. Venugopalan, (L) Prof. T. Ambrose are my constant motivators.

It would be incomplete if I do not include some special people of my life - Ima, my siblings and family members. Many of my friends are directly or indirectly involved in my journey as well - Nganba, Joshua, Bharatbhusan, Lenin, Romesh, Anjali, Nini and Murali.

My wife has always been my greatest strength. Along with Lishaang and Loushing, she made everything so easy for me.

CHAPTER I

Analyse

Every human being is unique in one way or another. This uniqueness might be due to genetic or environmental factors or both. However, there could be different personality types. Here, we are focusing on Ten Personality types.

Are you aware of your personality type? If yes, is that personality going to help you climb higher in career and life?

If not, you'll find out from this book.

Can you shift or change your personality? And if you do, will you become the same person?

Let's start with the ideas of different personalities. Don't worry! You have one to many of this personality in you.

CHAPTER II

The Egoist

Your attitude to life is simple and direct.

Every decision you make in life is based on one question – "What's in it for me?"

This type of personality is based on 'me first'.

You are selfish, greedy and ruthless.

If your personality hurt others, it cannot be good. Your desire for self-advancement, if it hurt other people should be work upon because you might end up being alone.

You are interested in yourself only. And when the next person does not serve you, you are not interested in the person at all.

During a crisis or any struggle, if it is not yours, you do not support it at all. You do not understand other people's situations, simply because that's not your situation.

You are not responsible for any situation, rather you blame the other person.

However, you want to be the centre of attention, and things to get done in your own way. And when you do not get what you want, you become stubborn.

You consider people who do not do things for you as selfish.

You are 'I think I'm better, I think I'm the best. I think I'm more important.'

If you face any criticism, the person is just ignorant. And if nobody praise you, they envy you because they do not have what you have.

This type of personality needs to be careful because the person is insecure. They always try to maintain certain image so no one discovers that they are fraud.

Any rejection to their decision, maybe from a person or community will blow their ego and they become maniacal.

CHAPTER III

The Egotist

You are boastful to the point of being obnoxious. You are too self-centered. When you are in a group, all you care is 'YOU'. You will talk about your achievements; boast about your conquests. You are an expert in practically everything!

You become too monotonous. What you think, what you have done, how good you are, how you would solve problems, etc. are all YOU only.

You are like – "I'm wonderful, come look at me."

This personality could be hazardous to other. Would you accept if your friend is too proud?

You are not modest, so people do not look upon you.

CHAPTER IV

The Altruist

5

You are a helper.

Your happiness lies with the welfare of other.

You concentrate more on helping others.

Sometimes, you forget your happiness and interest, because your personality wants to help the next person.

CHAPTER V

The Introvert

You are a living questionnaire.

You question all your acts.

But the questions are usually futile questions. How do I look? What would the other person think of me? Maybe he's hurt with me!

These thoughts constantly disturb you. You are unable to spend much time with other people because you fear that they might analyse you as you think.

You are not unsocial though because you always want to be liked and accepted.

You are usually shy and quiet, often moody and unhappy.

You prefer being solitary and at most you want a company of one person.

You tend to be more creative, but do not want co-operation with other people.

You may even be a genius or become one.

CHAPTER VI

The Extrovert

Quite contrary to Introvert, you would be a great teacher, preacher, counselor, administrator or a great orator.

You are always interested in other people's problems.

You are the heartthrob and centre of attraction of any gathering, because you never worry about the effect of your actions.

You never inhibit yourself with doubts about dignity.

You are always happy and tend to make others happy with your high spirits.

You love to be with people – lots of people.

CHAPTER VII

The Ambivert

You are a blend of introvert and extrovert.

You are a hybrid.

Your actions differ from time to time and on different occasions.

Your interests are usually in equal proportions, both being outward and inward.

You like both individual and group works.

You like being alone as much as being in a party.

You like to be the spotlight, at the same time being at the corner too.

Your personality is liked by all, because you blend everywhere.

CHAPTER VIII

The Misanthrope

You are cynical, i.e., you do not trust or respect the goodness of other people and their actions. Rather, you believe that people are interested only in themselves.

You are embittered and feel angry and unhappy because of the unpleasant and unfair things that happened to you or around you.

You are suspicious and hate everyone, especially yourself.

In other words, you hate human race.

You begin to explore the stupidity, meanness and the crookedness of almost all human.

CHAPTER IX

The Misogynist

You hate all women, girls included.

You discriminate women. And you could be a woman yourself too because you believe that you and your ways of life are superior to others.

You believe that women are no good at all.

You are arrogant.

You lack respect.

You are unable to keep promises or even manipulation.

CHAPTER X

The Misogamist

You do not want to make a legal commitment with the opposite sex.

According to you, the opposite sex is great as lovers, roommates, friends but never as a wedded spouse.

Wedding is too binding for you and commitment is deeper and more meaningful if freedom is available without any judicial norms.

You do not like wedding invitations and the ceremony following it.

Some misogamist hates the idea of being married, while others object the entire institution of marriage.

CHAPTER XI

The Ascetic

12

You always go into self-denial.

You are very strict and serious about yourself.

You consider self contemplation, that too lonely is good life.

You are self-controlled, purposeful and mindful with regards to consequences.

You consider simplest food and the least amount of it will keep your body and soul together.

You want abstinence from earthly pleasures and lead to spiritual perfection.

CHAPTER XII

The Choice

Let's enter into the next step.

What is the best personality type?

Well, this is a bad question because we have our own personalities. And this do not come so easily. This is a build-up of our experiences too. So, looking for an alternative personality is going to be tough, but not impossible. And having an alternative will allow us some freedom of choice. However, such an alteration imply that we change ourselves. Will you be ready to change yourself? Why not? That's for your own good. An alternate plan need not necessarily be inferior too. So, buckle up and get ready.

CHAPTER XIII

The Change

The topic 'The Change' itself is not satisfactory. It could have been the adaptation. There could be various ways, but today, I am considering The Eisenhower Matrix.

US President Dwight D. Eisenhower once said, "The most urgent decisions are rarely the most important ones."

Managing self requires discipline. Mastering self requires methods and techniques which are 'done and dusted' by several other 'people' who lived on this planet and are living now too. Several millions of people are with us together and several others passed away even before we were born. All of them have one to many 'personality'. They survived, some successful many not. Which one would you like to follow? Obviously, the successful ones.

Let's discuss the Eisenhower Matrix to bring a change or to adapt your personality according to the situation.

Begin by breaking down the job and decide how to proceed. We often focus strongly on the 'urgent and important' ones for they have to be dealt immediately. But ask yourself – How about the things that are important, but not urgent? When will you deal them?

If your current personality is not going to help you for the occasion/situation, that becomes 'urgent and important'. For a long run, say career, lifetime, etc. it becomes 'important but not urgent'. Do not forget, those 'important but not urgent' will eventually become 'important and urgent' in no time. So, take your decision wisely and change yourself suitably.

Some Good Books

A book is a gift you can open again and again. There are several books that could improve your personality. Some books are

1. Think Again by Adam Grant

Wharton psychologist Adam Grant offers bold ideas and rigorous evidence to show how we can embrace the joy of being wrong, encourage others to rethink topics as wide-ranging as abortion and climate change, and build schools, workplaces, and communities of lifelong learners.

2. As A Man Thinketh by James Allen

Allen describes how a man can change his life by changing his thoughts. We rise and fall in exact accordance with the character of the thoughts which we entertain. Our environment is the result of the thoughts that we harbor and the behavior that our thoughts bring about.

3. The Power of Positive Thinking by Norman Vincent Peale

Dr. Peale demonstrates the power of faith in action. With the practical techniques outlined in this book, one can energize one's life — and give oneself the initiative needed to carry out one's ambitions and hopes.

4. The 7 Habits of Highly Effective People buy Stephen R. Covey

Covey reveals a step-by-step pathway for living with fairness, integrity, service, and human dignity–principles that give us the security to adapt to change and the wisdom and power to take advantage of the opportunities that change creates.

5. You can Win by Shiv Khera

This book will help you to
· Build confidence by mastering the seven steps to positive thinking
· Be successful by turning weaknesses into strengths
· Gain credibility by doing the right things for the right reasons
· Take charge by controlling things instead of letting them control you
· Build trust by developing mutual respect with people around you
· Accomplish more by removing the barriers to effectiveness

6. The Magic of Thinking Big by David Schwartz

This book has step-by-step approach that will show you how to:
– Defeat disbelief and the negative power it creates
– Make your mind produce positive thoughts
– Plan a concrete success-building programme
– Do more and do it better by turning on your creative power

– Capitalise on the power of NOW

7. Mindset: The New Psychology of Success by Carol S. Dweck

Carol S. Dweck, Ph.D., discovered a simple but groundbreaking idea: the power of mindset. In this brilliant book, she shows how success in school, work, sports, the arts, and almost every area of human endeavor can be dramatically influenced by how we think about our talents and abilities.

People with a fixed mindset—those who believe that abilities are fixed—are less likely to flourish than those with a growth mindset—those who believe that abilities can be developed. Mindset reveals how great parents, teachers, managers, and athletes can put this idea to use to foster outstanding accomplishment.

8. How to Win Friends and Influence People by Dale Carnegie

How to Win Friends and Influence People recommend complimenting people honestly, smiling naturally, and genuinely taking an interest in their lives by asking questions. How to Win Friends and Influence People is a must-read for anyone looking to improve their soft skills or public speaking skills.

9. Think and Grow Rich by Napolean Hill

It offers valuable insights into the mindset and strategies required to achieve financial success and personal fulfillment. Hill's principles, such as desire, faith, persistence, and the power of the mastermind, provide a practical blueprint for anyone seeking to improve their life. The book is filled with real-life examples and actionable advice, making it a must-read for those looking to unlock their full potential and pursue their dreams.

10. Atomic Habits by James Clear

Atomic Habits presents a proven system for building good habits and breaking bad ones. The key to building lasting habits is focusing on creating a new identity first. Your current behaviors are simply a reflection of your current identity.